10 YEARS EARLY

The New Physicians Guide
To Retiring 10 Years Early

Roshan Ajanee CFP®, CPA, CSA, EA

Here's What's Inside...

Introduction

March 2014
Dallas, TX

One of the things I see when working with new Physicians for the last 20 years, is they spend 10+ years getting through medical school and getting all the licenses they need and then they have all the stress and pressures of setting up a successful practice. It's all very exciting and a very busy time for them.

There is so much going on and their time is so limited, they haven't stopped to take a moment and ask where is this all leading? They are busy working in their practice and starting a family so they put off doing any long term strategic retirement planning. They've been meaning to, but there is always something more pressing on the to-do list.

Because of this, I knew I had to set out to make being able to retire 10 years early, simple and straight-forward for my clients. The time involvement had to fit with their busy lives. And it needed to be easy to implement and not something that would be hard to follow through on.

This book is a result of that idea.

I created a plan to help physicians strategically plan for their retirement, but with an eye on their busy schedules and with very little effort by them - less time than it takes to sit through a movie in fact.

What follows is a conversation I had where I show you how to avoid the common mistakes I see new physicians make with setting up their practice and how to retire 10 years early if you avoid them, all with just 90 minutes of your time.

Enjoy the book!

I hope it changes the way you think about your retirement, and encourages you to get on the path to retiring 10 years before your peers.

Regards,

Roshan Ajanee

10 Years Early!

Susan: Good afternoon, this is Susan Austin and with me is Roshan Ajanee from Dallas, Texas. Welcome Roshan.

Roshan: Welcome Susan. Thank you so much for having me here.

Susan: Today we're going to be talking about The New Physicians' Guide to Retiring 10 Years Early. Is that really possible, 10 years early Roshan?

Roshan: Absolutely possible. It is very doable and it is being done by many of my clients. I'm very confident this works. It's definitely possible.

Susan: How long have you been helping physicians retire early?

Roshan: I started the financial side of my business in 1999 and became a CPA in 1993 so it's been 20 plus years on the CPA side. Helping my clients retire years earlier than they thought possible is the most exciting part of what I do.

Why Don't More Physicians Retire Early?

Susan: I bet. Let's dive in. Why don't more physicians retire early in your opinion? What are the roadblocks?

Roshan: Probably one of the biggest obstacles is the procrastination part of it, where people think retirement planning is something too big to tackle right now. They know they should be planning for their retirement, but many of them just don't get around to it. It's not the knowledge - they have a pretty good sense of what they need to do, but what is often missing is the action part of it. They are busy people and they want to get it handled, but they stall when taking action. That's probably the number one reason that it doesn't get done.

The good news is, once people come in and take the action, once they get into the plan, it's very easy. The biggest problem is to get started. Once they make a decision to get on track to retire early, then it becomes easy.

Susan: Can you clarify when you say "new physician" who do you mean? How long have they been in practice would you say?

Roshan: Generally once they become physicians, they are usually under some training; a lot of them have a specialty and they have to work under another doctor for some time. Once they are finished with that, many of them want to work in a hospital. Then I find, maybe after usually three to five years, physicians say I want to branch out and be on my own. When they say I want to start my own practice, I want to have a solo practice by myself; those are the physicians that I can help the most. If you are an employee of a hospital, then usually the hospital has a 401K and you're on the payroll and a lot of the retirement planning is handled for you.

The physicians I'm talking about have gone through their training, being under a position, being with the hospital for a year or two or three and then now they're starting their own practice. That's where they need help because they are very busy focusing on growing their own business and these retirement things are not foremost in their mind. They are generally 35-40 years old, which is a key time because as we'll get into in a bit, one of the keys to retiring early is to start planning early.

Susan: I see. They're busy focusing on building their practice and all of their time and energy is going into that. You're suggesting they need to take the time and stop and think ahead towards their retirement.

Roshan: Just like with a snowball effect where the earlier you start, the faster and bigger your snowball becomes towards the end, 35 is a good time to start. Pretty much as soon as you start your practice you should start thinking about retirement, and often they think they will tackle this issue later, when the practice is making more money. I'm here to tell them, you don't have to be making a lot of money to start. All the motivational speakers say you don't have to be great to start but you have to start to be great. The same principle applies in the financial timing part of it, you don't have to be rich to start getting rich, you just have to start to get rich.

I see it all the time. People think once I have $500,000 in income or a certain amount of savings, then I'll think about all these things. That's absolutely not the right approach. You could start with just a few thousand dollars but the key part is start now. Start as early as possible. That's the number one suggestion I would say for these physicians. Don't wait until some future event happens. Start now.

The 3 Mistakes New Physicians Are Making Which Delays Their Ability To Retire Early...

Susan: What mistakes do you see physicians making, in your experience, in not being able to retire early?

Roshan: Very good question. The way it works is these physicians are on their own. They have spent a significant amount of their life, literally the first 30 years of their life, studying to become doctors. Obviously their education, the time, the knowledge they have is very high. These physicians spend a lot and are working very hard starting their practice.

In fact, it's very common for me to hear from them they're working 18 hours a day. The upside though is, once they start billing that many hours into their practice, they start making good money and their income shoots up decently very fast. The downside, however, is since they have more income, more taxes kick in. Very often I hear of these physicians being shocked at their first really large tax bill. They are unprepared for what a large number they will be looking at paying. For example, as soon as you start crossing $100,000 income mark you are at 25% tax bracket and once you cross the $200,000 level of income, you start paying about 33% and pretty soon you hit a higher tax bracket at 39% and even 43% for some of the physicians once you cross the $400,000 mark.

Think about it, you go to school and work hard and set up your practice in your specialty. You make $400,000 and you're very excited, as all your hard work is finally paying off. The next thing you know

Uncle Sam comes in and takes away $150,000 to $200,000 in taxes, including your social security and all that. You're literally paying half of your money in income taxes. That becomes a very big challenge for most physicians. That first big tax bill is a real eye opener for them.

So that's probably the biggest mistake I see. They don't anticipate this tax bill and therefore they don't have the right business structure in place to help minimize the tax liability so they pay out of pocket a lot more tax than they should be. It's a big problem.

Focus on Wealth Creation, Not Just Income...

Susan: They think because they are making higher income, retirement will just fall into place.

Roshan: Exactly. That brings us to the second mistake I see all the time. I had my own radio show for eight years and during that time, one thing I saw over and over was people confusing income with wealth. They think once they have a larger income, it will naturally turn into wealth but that's not true. Income is never wealth. You work hard, so now you're making more income but your tax keeps going up. It gets to a point where you've got to start the planning and that's what we are talking about here. How can you retire early? The secret comes in when you start early and do the planning from day one so you can start saving for retirement before you pay taxes. That's the key part of this whole formula; you plan it right from the start.

Susan: Are you suggesting that although they make high income, there is a way they don't have to pay the high tax for the government? Is that what I heard you say?

Roshan: Yes, and that's the third mistake I see, paying too much tax. The way it works is, the more you make, the more your tax bracket goes up. But there's a perfectly legal way where you take some of the income from your top bracket and push that money to your retirement account, thus reducing your tax liability. You are in the 40% tax bracket, but you're saving at the higher bracket and putting money into your retirement account. You're actually doing two things here, reducing your tax liability but also funding your retirement. Those two things are key for retiring early, but you have to start planning.

Strangely enough, where physicians are concerned, their own good work ethic can actually work against them. They start pushing harder and working harder but what they often do is increase their tax liability. Without proper planning, this can backfire. It's a negative impact on their future if they are paying too much in taxes and not saving enough for their retirement.

Grow Taxes Into Wealth and Retire 10 Years Early...

Susan: Let me make sure I have this right. With proper planning, if they have high income, which is often the case with physicians, they don't need to pay so much in taxes. Divert the money which was going to the IRS and fund your retirement instead. I like it.

Is there a formula you use, to figure out how much income you set aside for this purpose? How do you know how much to divert to fully take advantage of this?

Roshan: Very good question. A simple formula, if you are making a lot less money, say $50,000 or less even then, you should be saving at least 10% of what you make a year. That goes for everyone, not just our physicians. Now once you start making $100,000 in income, then that percentage of saving should be at least 20%. Then for every $50,000 you earn, your percentage should go up by 5%.

So someone making about $200,000 should be saving 30%. At $400,000 you should be at 40%, and at half a million dollars you should be saving at least half of what you earn. It is very important because the more you make, the more your tax bracket goes up and the more you can save on your annual tax bill when can defer that payment at a higher tax bracket. For example, when a person in the 15% income tax bracket saves $17,500 in a retirement account, he cuts his tax bill by $2,625 vs. a person in the 39.6% tax bracket who cuts his tax bill by $6,930.

And when you do this, two things happen; your tax liability goes down and you pay less and less in taxes compared to what your income is or your taxes would have been. That's how this whole process works so you can retire 10 years earlier; divert the money you are paying to the IRS. Instead, start early and put that money to work for you. Put it towards your retirement and start building your future. It's a foolproof way to retire 10 years early.

Susan: Very good Roshan. That's pretty exciting. So a big part of your plan is taking money that would normally be paid to the government and using it to fund their retirement and as a result they can retire earlier than originally planned? What kind of timeframe are we talking about here? If they follow your plan and are able to retire 10 years early, do we have a range for how that looks?

Roshan: Absolutely, in fact I have a few physicians right now that are planning for their retirement and they're just about 50 years old. They want to retire in the next three to five years, which is very young, traditionally speaking, for doctors to look at retiring. It's a good age for these doctors. Imagine they have worked 30 years for studying, and when we say studying, we're not talking one hour a week. They're talking 100 hours a week they study. Once they get to work, they're working 100 hours week. They've never known anything else but work and study so to be frank, they deserve it.

I'm saying it's very possible for them to retire at 55, not that they don't have to work. It's just that they could decide that they don't want to work, and that makes all the difference.

Susan: They get to make the choice to keep working or not, and I assume you mean retire at their same lifestyle?

Roshan: The point of retirement is to have fun because at that age you are still young and you have all the energy to do everything you want. Many of these physicians are in very good health, and they keep themselves very well. They want to enjoy life and they are learning now, why wait till they're 75 and not be able to do anything?

What Happens When You Don't Have a Strategic Retirement Plan in Place?

Susan: That's key isn't it? Can you share an example with us of someone that you know without disclosing any confidentiality? Maybe someone that hasn't put a plan in place and what that looks like and what the ramifications of waiting too long is?

Roshan: In fact, I had a caller on my radio show and didn't know at the time, who turned out was a physician. He was asking a question and I was sharing some point on the air about how income is not wealth. I was just talking about it, as that was the topic of that day's show. How people work hard, they're pushing extremely hard all the time, all they think is I need to get more income. When I shared the phrase 'income is not wealth', this guy was shocked with that statement and he called me live on the air to discuss it.

After the show, he asked me more questions and then finally he stopped by my practice. We asked him, like we do for all our clients, some general questions for financial planning. We asked him, what do you do? He was almost 40 years old making more than $250,000 at that time as a physician. He had a very high income, a big house, a very nice expensive Mercedes Benz, a top new model with all amenities and luxuries you can think of but sadly, when we discussed his balance sheet, we discovered his net assets were less than $25,000.

How was it that someone making a multiple six-figure income could have such a low net worth? It was because he lacked a cohesive financial planning strategy. Many high income earners are in the same situation actually. This scenario was a very typical example of someone who thought they were wealthy because they had a comparatively high income and lifestyle, but income is not wealth. That was a huge wake up call for him. However, and this is key, since he had so much income, it was easy for us to show him how he can take that income, open a retirement account and start planning for his future.

The first thing we did was cut down his taxes. That was something that was very exciting to him as you can imagine. The next thing that happens is before you blink an eye, the money you diverted from the taxes added in with your savings which you're putting into your 401K, starts growing very fast. Recently we sat down to review things and he's one of those that I mentioned earlier - he's thinking of retiring in the next three to five years and it is very possible looking at the numbers because he has over $2 million in savings right now. Somebody who had nothing at nearly 40 years of age and now 12 years, 13 years later he's thinking of retiring by 56, which is absolutely doable.

Susan: That's exciting. He was headed down a very different path wasn't he?

Roshan: Yes but if he didn't make the call, chances are very slim that he would even be thinking about retirement at this point in time. Right now, he's probably 55 and he is very happy.

Here's Exactly How to Retire
10 Years Early...

Susan: How does this work Roshan? Can you explain how he was able to turn it around and look at retiring early when in fact he had so little 12 years ago?

Roshan: Sure. The IRS has rules and regulations that allow you to divert a significant amount of money to tax deferred vehicles that can greatly increase your wealth. By maximizing the dollars the IRS allows you to place in these tax deferred accounts, you minimize your tax liability. Everyone has a choice to pay the "ugly" income tax expense now or defer some of the tax and grow it into wealth. But not everyone is aware of this option.

A lot of the physicians I see are very good in their field of practice, but they don't have a good strategy to defer their taxes. Let's consider this scenario. A doctor, age 35, is the sole provider at his practice. He establishes his business as a corporation. His spouse is helping in the office. The business grosses $250,000 and the doctor pays himself a salary of $120,000 and a reasonable salary to the spouse. In 2013 the doctor and the spouse are each allowed to contribute $17,500 into a 401(K). So, $35,000 is taken off the doctor's $120,000 annual salary and the spouse's annual salary as their personal 401(K) contribution amounts.

They do not have to pay taxes on the $35,000 until they begin taking it from their retirement accounts during their retirement years. Because the doctor set up his business as a corporation, the corporation can contribute 25% of his salary or $30,000 to his

401(K). This is considered by the IRS as a deductible business expense for the corporation as a profit sharing 401(K) deduction. However, now the doctor has $47,500 contributed to his retirement account and he has not paid taxes on the $47,500. The doctor has just deferred approximately $19,000 of income tax. If the doctor did this for 30 years, assuming a reasonable 7% rate of return on his investment, he will end up with approximately $4,486,887. That's nearly $4.5 million. That is the power of disciplined savings along with the power of compounding interest and of course, deferring taxes.

The whole concept is based on taking money you would normally pay in tax and combining it with some of your expendable income. Now if you have credit card debt at an interest rate higher than 18%, then it would make more sense to first pay off the credit card debt and the high interest rate loans before implementing this retirement plan. However, if you have a mortgage at 4% and student loans at 3%, you should begin setting aside money for retirement while you are paying off those lower interest rate loans.

Anyone who pays income tax can benefit from this concept. This can be set up so there is a contribution on a month to month basis or it is automatically payroll deducted. The tax deferred money comes in and goes directly to their 401(K). It can be set up in such a way as to be a very customer friendly process.

Retiring 10 Years Early Is Possible for Anyone, But Especially for Physicians...

Susan: Any specific tips for physicians reading this who want to retire early?

Roshan: The first thing is, for anybody to retire early, not just physicians; you have to have income because that's the first step. For you to retire early it's very simple but people need to know that if you make good income, if done properly, the more income you have the earlier you can retire. People always ask when I do the radio show, what do you need to retire? And I tell them, it's actually very easy - I have a saying "learn more to earn more". For people who are not doctors that's the rule, educate yourself, become very good at a skill and learn more to make more, that's my answer.

For doctors, it's a very simple process. They already have high income so they do not struggle in this area. The second thing I tell my clients, which I've learned over my experience of 20 years helping people retire early, my simple answer to them is to save more money.

That's one thing people just don't get. It is not the income. People rush, people spend their lives rushing around, but if you ask nine out of ten people, they will say I don't know where my money goes. It just went away. Don't let that happen to you. You work hard to earn your money, but it seems in this country it's 10 times harder to save money. Everyone wants to live for today. Without saving, nothing happens. Let me boil it down for you. Aside from winning the lottery, you can't retire early if you don't have savings. The good news, however, is with my plan it's easier than you think.

We encourage everyone to start saving. When you save money when you're 35 or 40 years old, you're saving for possibly the next 30 or 40 years because you could be living to 85 and 90, who knows? That's very common nowadays.

How to Put Your Money to Work for You...

Susan: What do you recommend they do with the savings?

Roshan: Good question. You've got to put that money to work for you. How you invest for your retirement is very important.

You want your money to work so that while you're working in your practice, growing your business, at the same time your money is working to grow your wealth.

This is a key part in wealth accumulation. If you have a retirement plan which you start very early, Uncle Sam gives you certain limits every year that you can pour into your retirement plan in which you don't pay taxes.

You don't have to pay taxes till you decide when you want to take out that money. For many people that could be when they are more than 70 years old. That's where they start doing the required minimum distribution (RMD). To recap, it may seem simple but it's very powerful; over time, you make money, you save money, you invest your money and you invest in a tax deferred account, to get the best results. That's the formula for anyone to retire well and with my help I'm saying you can retire 10 years earlier than you may have planned for originally.

No One Likes to Pay Taxes...

Susan: This money that's growing through investment, that was tax deferred, will the government be standing there with their hand out wanting their piece of the pie when you go to use this money in retirement?

Roshan: Absolutely. If you have to write a $100,000 check to Uncle Sam and I say Susan, I'll give you a choice, would you rather write a $100,000 check today to Uncle Sam or would you rather write it 45 years from now? Obviously if I have that choice I'll write it 45 years from now or 40 years from now. I decide when I pay the taxes. Not everyone knows this, but you have the choice to defer your taxes, take that tax money and put into your retirement account, let it grow and when you decide, then you write a check at that time.

In truth, if you're really smart what you pay in taxes could be much less than what you pay right now. It all depends on the proper planning part of the formula. Just to give you an example, let's say today you're at 40% tax bracket and you are able to divert $100,000 into your 401K account which basically saves you $40,000 in taxes. Now time has gone by, you're 70 years old, you don't have any other income and now you take out that $100,000 to live on, you probably will not be in the 40% tax bracket.

You may be in a 20% tax bracket or 25% bracket because you still get exemptions. If done right you could only be paying 20% 40 years from now. Not the 40% when you put the money in. That's a huge savings and it's a big part of the formula.

Susan: So earn income, save money, invest wisely and best of all, divert money you're already sending to the government and use that money to fund your future. What does the structure look like? Did you say it was a 401K or it's not a 401K?

Roshan: Well, it is a 401K. It gets a little technical but it's very simple for some physicians who don't have many employees. A lot of times they start very small and they're just employing their spouse with them and don't have very many employees. They can do a solo 401K which is a single person solo 401K. That one is very easy to set up and very cheap. Then there's a 401K which if you are employing 5, 10 or 15 people, you could set up a retirement plan which could be monitored by third party administrators and we help them set this up, with the monitoring, the paperwork and everything.

That's basically a 401K. Once you start making even more money, then you could set up a retirement pension plan which is your employer set pension plan. That gets a little technical also but if you're in a very high tax bracket and you think you're going to have very high income, a pension plan really is very handy for many physicians.

Susan: I love what you said about income is not

wealth because I think interestingly enough a lot of people actually teach that your income is your number one wealth building tool. I hear that a lot in fact. You're actually saying yes and no. I don't want to put words in your mouth but you're saying, don't just assume because you are on track to making lot of money that that's going to get you where you want to go and have the choice to retire at 55 instead of 75.

Roshan: This is so true. I had a lady come to me. She had never made more than $30,000 a year in her life. She was 55 when she first came to me with $155,000 in savings. Now she's about 60 years old, and at this current time has over $200,000 saved. Then I talk to some of these physicians as I said before making $300,000 and more, and they only have $25,000 in their savings account. Believe me, income is not wealth. The most important part that most people forget is the saving part of it. If you have income, if you don't save it, it's not wealth. Income is not wealth.

Susan: I like though that you're proposing if you do it right and you set up the plan and the structure for your business a lot of that savings can come from money that you are going to write to the IRS anyway.

Roshan: That is correct yeah.

How Avoiding These Common Mistakes Will Help You Retire Early...

Susan: Let's switch gears and talk about the mistakes you see that stops people from retiring early.

Roshan: One mistake I see these guys make is waiting too long to start the process. There is a window to start maximizing how early they can retire and so starting early is key. Putting this off until the practice is more established is a big mistake in my opinion. Starting a retirement plan as soon as possible makes a big difference because the compounding of money is a very magical thing, so your few thousands which you save 30 years ago could be many thousands 30 years later. That's called the compounding of wealth.

Another key mistake, as I stated earlier, is thinking income is wealth; thinking that because they make or are on track to make a lot of money, somehow it will materialize into wealth. That's not the case.

Another important mistake I see people make is taking on too much risk. Once they have the savings, they think, "I can take this money and somehow make 110% return on my money". They think that's the best way to make me wealthy. I've seen people lose everything in real estate; people lose money in the stock market by trying to do very unusual things and trying to get and unreasonable amount of return.

Risking your money and trying to get unrealistic returns is the way most people ruin their chances of retiring early. Remember, return off the principle is more important than return on the principle.

Susan: Can you share an example of someone who made one of these mistakes? As you said, don't gamble with your nest egg.

Roshan: Absolutely. This guy Fred, he was over

50, this was around the 2000 time frame, right around the tech bubble. He had invested very heavily into some tech stocks. People who know the history of the stock market, may recall, some of those stocks went down 98%, so he lost in total about $2 million in the stock market. Sadly a couple of years prior, he was making $300,000 to $400,000 every year in the stock market. After the stock crashed, he had $200,000 left from $2 million and he came to me to see if he could write off all of those losses. He came to me for a tax review.

I explained to him, "No, the most you can write off is to take a $3,000 write off every year and it's probably going to be 200 years before you can fully write off those losses". That was a huge eye opener for what a bad risk the stock market can be. He didn't become my client; in fact, he was very upset with me for giving him the bad news. People lose life savings just taking an unreasonable amount of risk. He didn't need to risk his future that way to secure what he wanted, which was wealth for his family.

Susan: It's not worth it, right?

Roshan: Yeah absolutely. It's an important lesson we teach people - don't take on extra risk if you don't have to. You can get a good reasonable return in the market with diversifying into proper investments. That is a much better way than trying to beat or time the market. You should avoid high risk.

Susan: Even physicians, Roshan? They are on the more intelligent side of the scale, so to speak, so can't they invest in the market?

Roshan: You see the problem with the stock market is it's just not a logical place. Physicians are used to scientific process so they know exactly how one plus one becomes two. When they come to the stock market, there can be a stock that could have been worth $100 now selling for $1. It could go down so much and people just don't understand it. How can it be possible? That's how they lose a lot of money because they're very logical thinking people and the stock market doesn't always follow logic.

Sometimes I see physicians making bigger mistakes than say the average person who is not that highly educated because they're very logical people and the stock market is not logical.

Here's Exactly How to Get Your Retirement Plan in Place to Retire 10 Years Early...

Susan: Interesting. Switching gears now, how does the ten year early retirement plan work? Can you walk us through how someone can get involved?

Roshan: Absolutely. Over the years, one thing I have found to be very true of physicians is they are very busy. They just don't have a lot of time. So we set out and asked, how can we add value to doctors? How can we get them on the track to retiring 10 years early, but not need a lot of their time? We have created a process, which we have put many of our clients through.

We came up with this solution where we just need

90 minutes of their time. We sit down with the physicians and go over the whole process and after those 90 minutes literally everything about their retirement strategy is automated. We know when they leave our office; they are going to go back to their busy life, so we set it up so the process doesn't rely on them to make sure their retirement is secure. We get them out of their own way, so to speak. They come in, we go over everything and they sign a few papers and we take care of the rest. We handle the taxes for them. We handle their investments, everything from finding the right investments, and setting up the easy logins so that they can access their accounts. Everything is done at our back office without having to rely on the physician to get things done.

That's the number one thing I would say that we have put together for these physicians. We take the headache out of the process for them. Once they come in, we agree on the process and strategy that is best for them. We have the initial interview of 30 minutes where they come to see us, ask questions and decide if they like us and we like them. We have to agree and be on the same page.

The 10 Years Early Retirement Plan Can Give You Peace of Mind...

Roshan: Once we get through the initial meeting, we handle everything. We set up the accounts, do the paperwork filing and the payroll. We handle it all for them. Then going forward, we check in with them, but they don't need to keep coming back into the office. We can do call conferencing. They can rest easy that their retirement is being looked after and someone is looking out for their best interest. That is the best part, because they can go back to living their lives, knowing that there is a process in place to help them retire early. The biggest thing my clients tell me is once we finish the meeting, they have peace of mind for the first time.

Susan: That's pretty exciting. You're saying for those who have been putting this off because they think they just don't have the time dedicated to figure this all out, just give me 90 minutes of your time and you'll come in and get them started on this path to retiring a possible 10 years early.

Roshan: Absolutely. That's all it takes.

The 10 Years Early Retirement Plan Works Even if You've Employed the Services of a CPA...

Susan: If a physician is listening to this and they're interested but they already have a CPA or a tax accountant they work with is that okay?

Roshan: Absolutely. In fact many of my clients have already employed a CPA. That's fine. I'm also a CPA myself and I understand how valuable it is to have a good relationship.

If they have a CPA they are working with, that actually makes things easier. We still work with them to help them set up a retirement plan and monitor the investment part. A lot of CPAs are set to work in the short term, this year's filings and this year's income, but they don't always look 15 years down the road and ask where are we heading? What can we do now that can speed up this process? That's what I help them with. Working with their CPA is no problem. Absolutely it can be done.

Susan: Although retirement planning is complicated from the physician's point of view, they just need to book the appointment with you, come in and meet with you. You'll explain more of the details of how it works and then your team handles all of the details so they know it has been handled. I think that's amazing.

Roshan: Yes, as I said earlier helping these people get on a path to having a choice of retiring a lot earlier than they dreamed possible is the most exciting thing for me. If someone wants to get started, they can call our office at 972-484-0020 or they can go to our website 10yearsearly.com.

Susan: Very good Roshan. I think anyone who wants to retire early should make that call. Any last comments you want to make to these physicians that are listening and are intrigued about retiring earlier than their peers?

Roshan: Number one, I would again say don't worry that it's too difficult. It's a very easy process. Imagine 90 minutes now can save you 10 years of your life. The program works. It's working for other physicians and it can work for them.

Susan: Very good, very exciting. Thank you so much. Thank you for sharing this with us. It's a life changing idea. Why not put your money to work for you? Their money should be working as hard for them as they work for their patients. Thank you again Roshan.

Roshan: You're very welcome Susan. Thank you.

Here's How to Get Your 10 Years Early Retirement Plan in Place... in Just 90 Minutes...

You've been working hard setting up a practice and starting a family. When all of a sudden you get hit with an IRS tax bill you don't like. You've been meaning to meet with your CPA about this, but the time never seems to materialize to take a closer look at this. It's been a lingering item on your to-do list and one of these days you'll get to it.

Retirement is this vague notion off in the distance and there is always something else more pressing on your time. That is why we created the 10 Years Early Retirement Plan. We help people just like you create and document a plan to retire 10 Years Early... in as little as 90 minutes.

Step 1: We spend 30 minutes together making sure we are a fit for each other and fully address any questions you may have and go over the plan with you.

Step 2: We take you through a 60-minute in-depth questionnaire to document what you want your retirement to look like and when you want that to happen.

Step 3: We take it from there. Our team of experts does the due diligence required and we craft your 10 Years Early Retirement Plan so that you can go off and live your life and have the peace of mind about your retirement you've been craving.

Now you can get on the path to Retire 10 Years Early giving you what you really want – financial independence in as little as 90-minutes.

If you'd like us to help, just visit our website: www.10yearsearly.com and we'll take it from there.

www.ingramcontent.com/pod-product-compliance
Lightning Source LLC
Chambersburg PA
CBHW070729180526
45167CB00004B/1682